Come,

Follow Me

Mission: To Proclaim Transformation and Truth

Publisher: Transformed Publishing
Website: www.transformedpublishing.com
Email: transformedpublishing@gmail.com

ISBN: 978-1-953241-33-7 Paperback
ISBN: 978-1-953241-34-4 Hardcover

Come,
Follow Me

Dynisha Warren-Fresneda

Dedication

To my late pastor, Bishop Bud Mickins, thank you for the push into purpose. You have taught me to love and desire the will of God for my life. You have prepared me for such a time as this. Your influence and legacy will continue to live through every person who gleans from this book. You will forever be in my heart.

To my daughter, Aiyanna Fresneda and the many daughters who will read this book; arise and know your position in God. Be empowered to make Jesus your choice, so you won't settle for anything less. You are fearfully and wonderfully made.

Foreword

Written by Takela S. Golson

I have spent my entire life trying to be one with God and be who He has called me to be. I have looked far and wide for a word that will clearly tell me exactly how to do it. Beyond the Bible I have found that simplicity is the key.

Come, Follow Me has provided a simplicity of the word of God I did not know I needed. It has answered questions and confirmed God's voice to me in more ways than one. I will encourage you as you read through the pages of this book, to do so with a pen, notebook, and a still heart because through the words of this book, month by month, the Holy Spirit is speaking; and you want to listen.

Table of Contents

Fresh Start

It is time to start afresh. It is amazing that even before we go through or into a new year God has already established what will happen in our lives. Just think about it, your life's journey was ordained and established before the foundation of the world! God has always considered you and nothing concerning you surprises God.

> Before I formed thee in the belly I knew thee; and before thou camest forth out of the womb I sanctified thee, and I ordained thee a prophet unto the nations.
> -Jeremiah 1:5 KJV

Without a doubt we can stand firm with assurance that God knows us and is committed to walking with us on this journey. In fact, the Bible tells us God will never leave us nor forsake us.

> *Let your* conduct *be* without covetousness; *be* content with such things as you have. For He Himself has said, "I will never leave you nor forsake you."
> -Hebrews 13:5

In this new year you can become a new person. This doesn't necessarily mean your family, or your physical appearance will change, but your heart will change. In order to become this new person, you have to repent of your sins and confess with your mouth that Jesus is Lord and you will be saved.

[T]hat if you confess with your mouth the Lord Jesus and believe in your heart that God has raised Him from the dead, you will be saved.

-Romans 10:9

Through Salvation, the promises of God that belong to you come to pass.

For I know the thoughts that I think toward you, says the Lord, thoughts of peace and not of evil, to give you a future and a hope. Then you will call upon Me and go and pray to Me, and I will listen to you. And you will seek Me and find *Me*, when you search for Me with all your heart.

-Jeremiah 29:11-13

Children of God have access to Him through prayer. When you seek God to know His ways and to align your will to God's will, He will perpetually keep you this year and in years to come.

A Look in the Mirror

1. What are some plans you have for this year?

_____

_____

_____

_____

_____

_____

_____

_____

_____

2. Do your plans line up with the will of God?

_____

_____

_____

_____

_____

_____

_____

_____

*Additional planning and journaling space available beginning on page 75.

Something to Remember & Apply

This means that anyone who belongs to Christ has become a new person. The old life is gone; a new life has begun!

-2 Corinthians 5:17 NLT

Prayer:

God, thank You for a new year. Help me to grow closer to You through Your word. God help me to love You and know You for myself. Teach me how to live this year as Your new creation. I believe and receive all the promises You have given to me as a child of God. I ask that You help me to stay faithful and stand strong on Your word.

In Jesus name, Amen.

No Greater Love

We welcome anything that makes us feel loved: flowers, candy, balloons, etc. You may want to hear, "I love you," more from your significant other or may be awaiting a grand marriage proposal, but what if I told you that you are already loved. Loved far greater than any outward display of affection. More importantly, what if you believed you are loved with an everlasting eternal love from God. In this season, remember that you are worthy of unconditional love.

Before I got married the Lord revealed to me Ephesians 5:25.

> Husbands, love your wives, just as Christ also loved the church and gave Himself for her,
>
> -Ephesians 5:25

I thought to myself the degree of love my husband should have for me is deep. I began to fall intensely and intentionally in love with Jesus when I received the depth of love God has for me. That love instantly took root in my heart. I began praying and making the declaration that I will marry a man who loves me like Christ loves the church because I am entitled to be loved like that. At that moment, the bar was set. *I am not accepting anything less.*

Take hold of the word of God. He will fulfill it when you believe. My husband is Cuban, and his family is very close. Early in our marriage his brother and sister would tell me,

"You are just his wife, but we are his blood." I knew they lacked understanding. I also knew the enemy wanted to plant a seed, but I had the word God gave me hidden in my heart.

One day while we were all talking, my husband's sister randomly asked him if he would die for anyone. He answered, "Yes, I would die for my baby."

Our daughter was about three years old at the time, so my sister-in-law responded, "I know you would die for your daughter."

My husband looked at her very seriously and said, "I am talking about my wife. I'd die for her and no one else. Our daughter will see my example as I love her mom and know she, as well, should marry a man that's willing to die for her."

At that moment my heart was overjoyed because God is faithful.

> So shall My word be that goes forth from My mouth;
> it shall not return to Me void, but it shall accomplish
> what I please, and it shall prosper in the thing for
> which I sent it.
> -Isaiah 55:11

The word God gave me years before I got married came full circle out of my husband's mouth. God keeps His promises;

He must. While waiting for love, don't settle for just candy or balloons. Make a declaration that you want the love God has already established for you. This love does not harm. This love helps, speaks life, and does not condemn. I encourage you to take hold of *this* great love God freely gives.

A Look in the Mirror

1. What does the love of God mean to you?

_____

_____

_____

_____

_____

_____

_____

_____

_____

2. How do you want to be loved?

_____

_____

_____

_____

_____

_____

_____

_____

_____

_____

3. How do you show love?

_____

_____

_____

_____

_____

_____

_____

_____

_____

4. Are you ready for love? Why or why not?

_____

_____

_____

_____

_____

_____

_____

_____

_____

*Additional planning and journaling space available beginning on page 75.

Something to Remember & Apply

Be anxious for nothing, but in everything by prayer and supplication, with thanksgiving, let your requests be made known to God;

-Philippians 4:6

Pray and boldly ask God for what you want. Pray His word and His promises because they are yours.

Prayer:

God, thank You for loving me with an everlasting love. I receive Your love into my heart. Saturate me so that love flows freely in and out of me. Help me get into position to receive love from the man You will send to me. Protect and preserve him. Lord, give him a heart that submits to Your will. Teach him Your ways and teach him how to love me. Give him grace, good understanding, and wisdom to lead.

In the mighty name of Jesus, Amen.

Seperate and Satisfied

Sunday after Sunday, Bible study after Bible study, youth group after youth group; this may seem repetitious and reduced to *just* a part of your weekly routine. What you don't see, is that this is preparation, preparation for your future in God. As you come to church and hear God's word being taught, know that every word is a seed being planted in your heart. You may not recognize this is happening, but God is laying a foundation of truth for you to build upon.

As a child my mom often said to me, "You can't go everywhere, nor can you do everything everyone else does." The way she said it always hinted something bad was going to happen to me. That used to bother me because I thought, *If everyone is going why would something bad happen to me, especially when there are tons of other people around?*

Now that I am older and God has opened my spiritual eyes, I know her not allowing me to go everywhere and not allowing me to do everything, was an attempt to keep me from being contaminated by ungodly influence.

> Therefore, "Come out from among them and be separate, says the Lord. . ."
> -2 Corinthians 6:17

Whether you know it or not, your parents and church family are praying for you. Even as a teenager, God is calling you to come out from among your peers and separate yourself so they will see the light of God in you.

Not only does God know your future; the devil also knows it. When you obey God and purpose in your heart to live for Christ the devil is waiting for an opportunity to get you in the wrong place at the right time to shift your destiny. So, *NO!* You can't go everywhere nor do everything!

Being different is not always easy. Some friends won't invite you to certain events or to hang out. That's not a good feeling but when this happens remember 2 Timothy 2:12 says, "If we endure, we shall also reign with *Him*." Be happy knowing that when you suffer for Christ Jesus you have something *more* eternal to look forward to, and that's reigning in heaven with Jesus forever in His presence.

A Look in the Mirror

1. Do you feel God has given you an urge to be different? If so, different in what way?

_____

_____

_____

_____

_____

_____

_____

_____

2. Do you think it's important to be different in front of your friends? If so, why should you let them see who you are?

_____

_____

_____

_____

_____

_____

_____

_____

*Additional planning and journaling space available beginning on page 75.

Something to Remember & Apply

I will give you a new heart and put a new spirit within you; I will take the heart of stone out of your flesh and give you a heart of flesh. I will put My Spirit within you and cause you to walk in My statutes, and you will keep My judgments and do *them.* Then you shall dwell in the land that I gave to your fathers; you shall be My people, and I will be your God.

-Ezekiel 36:26-28

God has called us to live holy lives, not impure lives.

-1 Thessalonians 4:7 NLT

Prayer:

Lord, create in me a clean heart and renew the right spirit in me. God, give me boldness to be different and unashamed. Help me to be an example before my friends and family so You are glorified in heaven. Thank You God, for calling me out to be different and set apart to be used by You as a light for my peers.

In Jesus name, Amen.

Teaching Toxicity

Shannon laughed as she talked on the phone with her best friend Casey, "Girl, you are so funny! Candace's hair was a mess, and her clothes were so ugly. No one likes her," as she motioned to her little sister Abbey to leave her room. "Casey, girl did you see her shoes? They were so dirty and dusty. I don't know why she would wear those."

Words are very powerful! It's important to know that what you say has the potential to hurt someone. We have all heard the saying, "sticks and stones may break my bones, but words will never hurt me." This saying is not true because your words can hurt more than sticks and stones. They can hurt emotionally and mentally, cutting so deep that someone could be damaged for life all because of something you said.

But no man can tame the tongue. *It is* an unruly evil, full of deadly poison.

-James 3:8

Death and life *are* in the power of the tongue, and those who love it will eat its fruit.

-Proverbs 18:21

Why does God warn us of the damages our words cause? God is giving us insight to the depth of the destruction our words can cause. In the scenario, the older sister Shannon is on the phone making fun of a classmate who is less fortunate than her friend Casey and herself, while Abbey her little sister is listening.

Do you think Shannon is instructing her little sister Abbey to go to school the next day and make fun of her own classmates? No, she has not directly instructed her to do so, but her actions suggest to her little sister that it is okay to make fun of someone.

As an older sibling, you are a person of influence. You have to set an example for those who are watching and are easily influenced by your actions to display the same toxic behavior. You never want to use your influence to encourage your siblings, friends, or family members to hurt others. The same way the things you say have the potential to hurt, what you say can also be used to edify and encourage others.

Using the same scenario, Shannon could have told her friend Casey it wasn't nice to *talk down* about someone who is less fortunate. Instead, they could have strategized ways to help her. For example, both girls could have asked their parents to intervene and purchase clothes, or even donate some of their gently used clothes and shoes to their classmate.

God is calling us to be the light in this dark world. Matthew 5:14 says, "You are the light of the world. A city that is set on a hill cannot be hidden." The only way for you to become light is to repent and ask God for forgiveness of your sins.

Once you have made the commitment to follow Jesus as your Savior, through His word (the Bible), He will teach you how to be a light who brings glory to Him.

Let your light so shine before men, that they may see your good works and glorify your Father in heaven.
-Matthew 5:16

The good you display may inspire someone to want what you have and that's Jesus Christ.

A Look in the Mirror

1. In what ways have you displayed toxic behaviors towards others?

_____

_____

_____

_____

_____

_____

_____

_____

_____

_____

_____

2. Who sees you when you are toxic towards others and what influence do you have over this person?

_____

_____

_____

_____

_____

_____

_____

_____

_____

_____

_____

3. How can you eliminate your toxic behavior?

_____

_____

_____

_____

_____

_____

_____

_____

_____

_____

_____

_____

_____

*Additional planning and journaling space available beginning on page 75.

Something to Remember & Apply

Just because you aren't talking,
doesn't mean you aren't teaching.

Do to others as you would like them to do to you.

-Luke 6:31 NLT

Prayer:

Heavenly Father, thank You for the lives I influence. Thank You for entrusting me with such a task. Give me a burden for those I influence. Help me to walk upright before You to show them You have the power to keep me from falling. God, give me grace for the precious lives of others. Help me to be a good example so my light shines and I help win souls for our kingdom.

In Jesus name, Amen.

In His Presense

Have you ever had something good happen to you and you respond, "Thank you Jesus!"? Then something else happens that is really good and you say, "Surely God is blessing me!"? Although good things happen, they are not enough and certainly do not confirm a relationship with God. It is important *not* to get caught up believing that good things alone are confirmation God is with you, therefore you must be good with God.

The latter part of Matthew 5:45 KJV says, "for he maketh his sun to rise on the evil and on the good, and sendeth rain on the just and on the unjust." That Scripture shows us blessings from God do not equal a relationship with God.

I was talking with my sister, listening to her rave about her business plans. Excitedly she shouted that she knew this business plan was from God. She was adamant He was going to bless her through this God-ordained business plan. Immediately I heard the Lord tell me to ask her, "But what about knowing Me?" I let out a huge sigh because I knew what her response would be.

Out of obedience, I began to share with her what the Lord said, and of course she quoted me the same Scripture, Matthew 5:45. She continued and said, "I don't have to be saved for God to bless me." My response was, "That may be true, but what good is it to only be blessed by God yet never experience the presence of God."

God's sovereignty, His righteousness, and His promises belong to the children of God. In the presence of God is where we meet the will and purpose of God. After our conversation I asked God to confirm what He had me to speak out loud. Later that day, I was studying the book of Isaiah and the Lord gave me His confirmation.

> Let favor be shown to the wicked, yet will he not learn righteousness; in the land of uprightness will he deal unjustly, and will not behold the majesty of the Lord.
>
> -Isaiah 26:10 KJ21

We must be careful *not* to miss the majesty of God, His splendor and greatness. Even when He has extended His hand of mercy and still you are blind and will not come to repentance; in that place you have missed God. Sure, you have a good blessing, but you have missed the opportunity to respond to the grace of God.

When we get into God's presence, He gives us spiritual blessings that are necessary to do the will of God effectively. Even if you never get a tangible blessing, you have something more when you have a relationship with God. Relationship comes with *access* in the presence of God. Don't get so consumed with blessings because Psalms 16:11

says, "You will show me the path of life; in Your presence *is* fullness of joy; at Your right hand *are* pleasures forevermore."

God is not short of blessing, but we need the presence of God more than blessings from God. In His presence is fullness of joy. The bible declares in Nehemiah 8:10, "...for the joy of the Lord is your strength." *This* strength helps us to endure.

For out of His fullness [the superabundance of His grace and truth] we have all received grace upon grace [spiritual blessing upon spiritual blessing, favor upon favor, and gift heaped upon gift].

-John 1:16 AMP

A Look in the Mirror

1. Why is it important to spend time in the presence of God?

_____

_____

_____

_____

_____

_____

_____

_____

_____

_____

_____

2. What does the majesty of God mean to you?

_____

_____

_____

_____

_____

_____

_____

_____

_____

_____

_____

_____

_____

3. How do you see God when the blessings are not coming?

_____

_____

_____

_____

_____

_____

_____

_____

_____

_____

_____

_____

*Additional planning and journaling space available beginning on page 75.

Something to Remember & Apply

The presence of God is where we should be. Seek Him.

Now therefore, I pray, if I have found grace in Your sight, show me now Your way, that I may know You and that I may find grace in Your sight. And consider that this nation *is* Your people."

And He said, "My Presence will go *with you,* and I will give you rest."

Then he said to Him, "If Your Presence does not go *with us,* do not bring us up from here. For how then will it be known that Your people and I have found grace in Your sight, except You go with us? So we shall be separate, Your people and I, from all the people who *are* upon the face of the earth."

So the LORD said to Moses, "I will also do this thing that you have spoken; for you have found grace in My sight, and I know you by name."

-Exodus 33:13-17

Prayer:

Lord, I don't want Your blessings more than I want You. Blessings are good but they are not eternal. Cultivate in me a desire for Your presence in my life. Teach me how to connect to You, seeking Your face and not just Your hand. Keep me in Your presence God, so I am led by You into Your perfect will.

In Jesus name, Amen.

A Relational God

Throughout our lives, we will be a part of many relationships. For example, you are someone's child, so there is the parent/child relationship and being someone's friend, in turn, creates a friendship. These examples represent different types of relationships we are a part of, each having specific roles and responsibilities.

As children, the Bible charges us according to Ephesians 6:1, "Children, obey your parents in the Lord, for this is right." So, we can gather the role and responsibilities of children are to obey their parents. When children obey their parents, they are also obeying God because He said *this* is right.

When we think of God, often we picture Him up in the sky ruling the heavens, untouchable and unconcerned with our day-to-day lives. Well, that thought is far from the truth! God is here with us, waiting to be invited into every area of our lives.

The Bible is full of great men and women who had relationships with God. Those men and women experienced hard times, including suffering. When they prayed to God, He heard them. This is the kind of access we have to God right now; as He heard them, He will also hear us. He is "a very present help in trouble," as confirmed in Psalms 46:1.

There was a king in Judah named Hezekiah, who served God well, "For he held fast to the LORD; he did not depart from following Him, but kept His commandments, which the LORD had commanded Moses." (2 Kings 18:6).

King Hezekiah kept the commandments of God, yet he became sick and was going to die. God sent the prophet Isaiah to deliver these words, "Thus says the LORD: 'Set your house in order, for you shall die, and not live.'" (*see* 2 Kings 20:1). King Hezekiah began to weep and pray to God, bringing to remembrance how he had served the Lord with a perfect heart. Before Isaiah could leave the king's courtyard, the Lord answered King Hezekiah's prayers and instructed Isaiah to tell King Hezekiah, "I have heard your prayer, I have seen your tears; surely I will heal you. On the third day you shall go up to the house of the LORD. And I will add to your days fifteen years." (*see* 2 Kings 20:5-6).

This account from the life of King Hezekiah, gives us insight to the relationship he had with God. Being so close to God that he could change His mind, shows the level of intimacy the king had with God. We can now see how good it is to be in an intimate and intentional relationship with God. Learning God's will through His word, as well as, learning what He loves and what He hates, helps build this deep intimacy with God. When you get to *this* place with God, allowing Him to rule and reign in your life, you will boldly ask and God will hear and answer you.

A Look in the Mirror

1. Do you think it's important to have a personal relationship with God? Why or why not?

_____

_____

_____

_____

_____

_____

_____

_____

_____

2. What does your current relationship with God look like?

_____

_____

_____

_____

_____

_____

_____

_____

_____

_____

_____

_____

_____

_____

3. How can you improve your relationship with God?

_____

_____

_____

_____

_____

_____

_____

_____

_____

_____

_____

_____

_____

_____

*Additional planning and journaling space available beginning on page 75.

Something to Remember & Apply

Relationship - the state of being connected.

STAY CONNECTED TO GOD!!!

Nevertheless the solid foundation of God stands, having this seal: "The Lord knows those who are His," and, "Let everyone who names the name of Christ depart from iniquity."

-2 Timothy 2:19

Blessed *are* those who hunger and thirst for righteousness, For they shall be filled.

-Matthew 5:6

Prayer:

Lord, help me to build a relationship with You. Give me a heart that loves and desires You. Let me see and understand that I need a relationship with You, so when I pray You will hear me and answer me. Teach me how to serve You, keeping Your will ever before me. Give me a thirst for Your word that will not depart from me.

In Jesus name, Amen.

Blessed in a Broken Place

We all have bad days, sad days, or days where nothing seems to go right. In these seemly difficult times for us, how do we see the God-given *good* we so desperately need? Psalms 62:8 encourages us to, "Trust in Him at all times, you people; pour out your heart before Him, God *is* a refuge for us. *Selah.*" It's wonderful that during our hardest moments, God gives us His listening ear. We may not feel like talking to our parents or friends, but we can always talk to God.

Prayer is a precious place where we can pour out the issues we face directly to God. Through prayer we build our relationship with God. Not only do we communicate with Him, but He also communicates with us. The latter part of the Scripture refers to God as a *refuge* which means in Him there is a safe place for us. In this safe place, we can escape the judgement of our bad decisions and be vulnerable to the pain we feel while being comforted by God's presence.

Praying opens this two-way communication where we are pouring out our hearts to God and He is simultaneously filling us up. Think about it like this, as we are pouring out, emptying, and letting go, space becomes available for God to fill up with His will. Then we can start to put His will into practice in our own lives.

A Look in the Mirror

1. What are some problems you are dealing with?

_____

_____

_____

_____

_____

_____

_____

_____

_____

2. When are good times for you to pray and why are those times the right times?

_____

_____

_____

_____

_____

_____

_____

_____

_____

*Additional planning and journaling space available beginning on page 75.

Something to Remember & Apply

*Prayer is simply talking to God about
something He already knows but
prefers to hear from you.*

Prayer:

God, teach me how to pray. Open my eyes that I might see the changes and effects of my prayer. Teach me how to be open before You. Pouring out all the burdens I carry so You can fill me up and equip me to carry out Your will for my life.

In Jesus name, Amen.

The Model Prayer
Our Father

". . .For your Father knows the things you have need of before you ask Him. In this manner, therefore, pray:

> Our Father in heaven,
> Hallowed be Your name.
> Your kingdom come.
> Your will be done
> On earth as *it is* in heaven.
> Give us this day our daily bread.
> And forgive us our debts,
> As we forgive our debtors.
> And do not lead us into temptation,
> But deliver us from the evil one.
> For Yours is the kingdom and the power and the glory forever. Amen.

"For if you forgive men their trespasses, your heavenly Father will also forgive you. But if you do not forgive men their trespasses, neither will your Father forgive your trespasses.["]

-Matthew 6:8-15

Total Surrender

"It's my life! I choose what I want to do with it! When I turn eighteen, I will be grown, and no one will tell me what to do!"

These statements have been made countless times by so many young people who are prematurely proclaiming their independence. These bold statements illuminate the strong will and mindset of the person. We all have a will we want to fulfill and be in charge of. For example, some may say, "If I don't want to do it then I'm not doing it." Or, "That is just the way I feel."

The culture of the world today says, "If you want to do it, then do it, because what you want for your life is your business and no one else should be bothered by it." In fact, people on social media encourage and applaud this attitude. DO NOT be deceived, this is NOT *who* you are!

And be not conformed to this world: but be ye transformed by the renewing of your mind, that ye may prove what is that good, and acceptable, and perfect, will of God.

-Romans 12:2 KJV

You cannot conform. There is purpose in you that is greater than what the world can ever offer you. Cell phones, social media platforms, and new clothes and shoes are not eternal.

Phones break, technology is ever-changing, shoes and clothes wear out, but following Jesus gets better and better. You must lay down your will.

> And he said to them all, If any man will come after me, let him deny himself, and take up his cross daily, and follow me.
>
> -Luke 9:23 KJV

You cannot do what you want to do! You must be contrary to the culture of the world. Deny your will and choose to follow the will of God for your life. God needs people who are concerned about His will and sincere about obeying His word.

A Look in the Mirror

1. What does it mean to surrender totally to God?

_____

_____

_____

_____

_____

_____

_____

_____

_____

_____

2. How and why should you deny your will?

_____

_____

_____

_____

_____

_____

_____

_____

_____

_____

*Additional planning and journaling space available beginning on page 75.

Something to Remember & Apply

Let it go and give it to Jesus.

Jesus said, "My food is to do what God wants Me to do and to finish His work.

-John 4:34 NLV

Prayer:

Lord, help me to choose to follow Your will for my life. Give me strength to deny myself, so that You are glorified in heaven. Guide my decisions and choices, reveal to me what Your good and perfect will looks like. God, teach me how to surrender to Your will so I can be used by You.

In Jesus name, Amen.

Sacrificial Worship

And Abraham said to his young men, "Stay here with
the donkey; the lad and I will go yonder and worship,
and we will come back to you."

-Genesis 22:5

This is a familiar account from the Bible for those who grew
up going to Sunday school. The breakdown is this, God told
Abraham that he and Sarah, his wife, would have a son.
Abraham and Sarah were already old in age. So old that
Sarah laughed at the idea of an old woman and a dried-up
old man giving birth to a child. Nevertheless, just as the Lord
spoke, Isaac was born.

God asked Abraham the unimaginable. Offer Isaac as a
sacrifice unto God. According to the Scripture, Abraham
saw sacrificing his only son as a chance to worship God. In
our lives, God is still asking for *this* sacrificial worship. He
wants us to offer *that* thing closest to our hearts to Him in
obedience. I'm speaking of the secrets you're holding on to,
or the relationship that is so important. Yes, God wants *that*!

Abraham understood, worship is not something you say but
rather something you do. God wants you to trust Him with
everything He gave to you; He requires all that you have.

Then they came to the place of which God had told him. And Abraham built an altar there and placed the wood in order; and he bound Isaac his son and laid him on the altar, upon the wood. And Abraham stretched out his hand and took the knife to slay his son.

But the Angel of the LORD called to him from heaven and said, "Abraham, Abraham!"

So he said, "Here I am."

And He said, "Do not lay your hand on the lad, or do anything to him; for now I know that you fear God, since you have not withheld your son, your only *son,* from Me."

-Genesis 22:9-12

Sacrificial worship puts us in the presence of God where nothing is hidden from Him; complete vulnerability before Him. When the angel spoke from heaven saying, "now I know that you fear God," the word *fear* is interpreted as reverence. To adore, honor, and obey God at His every command puts us in position to be blessed by God.

God promised Abraham that He would bless him. All he had to do was have faith and trust God. The same is true for us. We must have faith, trust God, and relinquish all we have in total surrender as a sacrifice unto God. Remember, Abraham called sacrificing his son an act of worship. Out of obedience we give God our worship. No matter what God asks us to do;

when we do *it*, we are worshiping God. This is something we must do daily. In today's society, God is not asking us to offer animals as He required in the Old Testament. He's asking for an offering of obedience.

> "What is more pleasing to the LORD: your burnt offerings and sacrifices or your obedience to his voice? Listen! Obedience is better than sacrifice, and submission is better than offering the fat of rams.["]
> -1 Samuel 15:22 NLT

We can do all the things that seem correct in the eyes of man when it comes to what society deems as religious or what a Christian *should* be doing, such as, going to church, Bible study, or praying. All good and necessary things; but will you give God your unconditional unrestrained, *yes*? Will you hold on to God, holding nothing back? Will you move when He says go? Will you release what's dear to you? Will you pick up the will of God with urgency!? God is looking for intimacy from you. He wants to trust that even if He calls for *that* issue near to your heart, you will obey and freely give.

A Look in the Mirror

1. What is the hardest thing God has asked you to give to Him?

_____

_____

_____

_____

_____

_____

_____

_____

_____

2. What is something you know you need to give to God?

_____

_____

_____

_____

_____

_____

_____

_____

_____

3. What makes the decision to obey God so difficult?

_____

_____

_____

_____

_____

_____

_____

_____

_____

4. Do you think there is a blessing when you obey God?
Why or why not?

_____

_____

_____

_____

_____

_____

_____

_____

_____

*Additional planning and journaling space available beginning on page 75.

Something to Remember & Apply

*Our bodies are a living sacrifice so every
day is an opportunity to worship.*

. . . [T]he Lord's delight is in those who fear him,
those who put their hope in his unfailing love.

-Psalm 147:11 NLT

Prayer:

Lord, I love You. I freely give of myself. All I have is Yours.
All my worship belongs to You. Teach me to worship You
in the beauty of Your holiness so I'm counted worthy in
Your sight. Release the well of worship inside of me so that
I'm a living sacrifice, holy and acceptable unto You.

In the name of Jesus, Amen.

Be Not Deceived

When you hear, "It's fall ya'll," what comes to mind? Fall festivals and kids excitedly dressing up in their costumes, playing games, and gathering sweet treats?

As we get older, dressing up may not be so fun anymore but if there is free food and candy, sign me up! During fall, the world celebrates Halloween, dressing up like ghosts, ghouls, and goblins. Everyone is getting ready for Halloween parties, not knowing whether they will get tricked or get a treat.

I want you to know something, a lot of people have been tricked. There is a deceptive spirit that has convinced many people they are *good* people and that's enough. A very good friend of my sister told me she wants, "a saved good godly husband." She went on to say that he must love God and attend church. I asked her if she was saved and she said, "No..., but I'm a good person. I may love partying and dancing, but I give to the poor and teach my kids to be nice people."

This conversation exhibited how many people think. The enemy has cunningly deceived so many people into thinking we can work our way into heaven but that is *not* true!

After letting my sister's friend speak her peace I asked her, "What makes you think a good godly man is looking for someone like you?" I could discern the shift in the conversation because she truly felt she was deserving of this type of man. I then asked her if she were to die, where did she think she would go, heaven or hell? She responded, "Honestly, I don't know because I'm not a bad person."

That response didn't answer my question, but it did indicate that she thought because she was a *good* person, she would not go to hell. She also knew, in her current condition, she was not prepared for heaven neither. So, I asked her why she put such a high priority on having a good Christian man, since by her own admission she was not a Christian woman.

This conversation highlights how often we place priority in the wrong place. We esteem relationships with our significant others or friends higher than the fact that we *need* God! The devil has deceived us into thinking we are good just the way we are and the decision to give our life to God is not important.

Yes, God wants you to have an abundant life, and a wonderful godly spouse who loves you; but ultimately those things are secondary. Receiving Jesus Christ in your heart must be *the* primary priority. The Bible says in Matthew 6:33 KJV, "But seek ye first the kingdom of God, and his righteousness; and all these things shall be added unto you."

We must be careful not to give priority to secondary issues. Dating or marrying the right guy, having good friends, and striving for excellency are important but they are secondary issues. We have many promises from God that ensure our needs and wants are taken care of. We must keep in the forefront of our mind that our priority must be God first, so we are not deceived and weighted down with the cares of this world.

> Delight yourself also in the Lord, and He shall give you the desires of your heart.
>
> -Psalm 37:4

> . . . no good thing does he withhold from those whose walk is blameless.
>
> -Psalm 84:11 NIV

> The thief does not come except to steal, and to kill, and to destroy. I have come that they may have life, and that they may have *it* more abundantly.
>
> -John 10:10

> But I fear, lest somehow, as the serpent deceived Eve by his craftiness, so your minds may be corrupted from the simplicity that is in Christ.
>
> -2 Corinthians 11:3

God knows what you want and need. I challenge you to put down what you want and pick up what God wants. Then you will begin to see God fulfill your desires according to His will.

A Look in the Mirror

1. What are some good qualities about yourself you think God would be pleased with?

_____

_____

_____

_____

_____

_____

_____

_____

_____

2. Are those good qualities enough for you to go to heaven? Why or why not?

_____

_____

_____

_____

_____

_____

_____

_____

_____

3. What are three short term goals you want to accomplish?

_____

_____

_____

_____

_____

_____

_____

_____

_____

_____

_____

4. How does God fit into those goals? Or does He?

_____

_____

_____

_____

_____

_____

_____

_____

_____

_____

*Additional planning and journaling space available beginning on page 75.

Something to Remember & Apply

When I was younger my grandmother used to tell me, "You are too good for hell but not good enough for heaven."

Just going to church or considering ourselves religious, does not give us access to heaven.

> But be doers of the word, and not hearers only, deceiving yourselves.
>
> -James 1:22

Prayer:

Heavenly Father, help me to never be deceived. Open my eyes so I am not blind to the subtle tricks of the enemy. Your word declares, "all our deeds of righteousness are like filthy rags" (*see* Isaiah 64:6 AMP). Help me present myself fully to You. Lead me into righteousness. Lord, keep me in pursuit of Your will so I may receive every promise from You.

In the name of Jesus, Amen.

True Worship

Shadrach, Meshach, and Abednego answered and said to the king, "O Nebuchadnezzar, we do not fear to answer thee in this matter.
If it be so, our God whom we serve is able to deliver us from the burning fiery furnace, and He will deliver us out of thine hand, O king.
But if not, be it known unto thee, O king, that we will not serve thy gods, nor worship the golden image which thou hast set up."

-Daniel 3:16-18 KJ21

Will you be counted as one who can truly worship God? Is your heart pure and your hands clean? A true worshipper doesn't need to see to believe, but they believe because they can spiritually see.

Let's look at the Hebrew boys encounter with King Nebuchadnezzar. The king made a decree that at the sound of the music everyone must bow to the golden image he created.

When it comes to worship, don't exalt any person because of their title, higher than God. It doesn't matter who's watching nor what they think. It is God who deserves our worship and it is God who we shall esteem higher than our dire circumstances.

Those young boys were facing the fire seven times hotter, yet they answered the king, "O Nebuchadnezzar, we do not fear to answer thee in this matter." The fact that they reverenced the true and living God higher than any earthly authority tells me they understood true worship.

Even when it's not comfortable, I still give God my worship because He is my priority. Yes, King Nebuchadnezzar can throw me in the fire, but all authority belongs to God who created the fire.

The Hebrew boys said our God is able to save us from this fire but if He don't, we still won't bow to the golden image. Ultimately in worshipping God, we *must* know our worship is not conditional, "If God shows up for me then I'll worship Him," - NOT SO!

We worship whether He shows up or not because we know that He is able. When we worship God things begin to shift in the spiritual realm to bring manifestation into the natural realm.

The boys knew worship is to be reserved for our God and the golden image cannot glory in our God's worship. Jesus Himself showed up in the midst of the fiery furnace and continues to show up for us in *every* fire. Our expectation must be, *when we worship God will show up!*

["]But the hour is coming, and now is, when the true worshipers will worship the Father in spirit and truth; for the Father is seeking such to worship Him. God *is* Spirit, and those who worship Him must worship in spirit and truth."

-John 4:23-24

Are you a true worshipper? In today's society many people say they are a Christian or know the Bible. There is a distinction between someone who *knows* the Bible and someone who consciously makes an effort to incorporate sound doctrine into their life. There is also a perversion the enemy wants to attach to worship; deceiving people into thinking worship is a facial expression, attire, or if I throw my hands up and my head back, I am worshipping. The Lord knew this deceit would be here, so He has called worshippers higher! You cannot fake worship. Your spirit must have a relationship with God to partake in acceptable true worship.

A Look in the Mirror

1. Can God count on your worship?

_____

_____

_____

_____

_____

_____

_____

_____

_____

_____

2. What does your worship look like?

_____

_____

_____

_____

_____

_____

_____

_____

_____

_____

_____

_____

_____

_____

3. Based on your previous answers, is it enough or how can you improve your worship to God?

_____

_____

_____

_____

_____

_____

_____

_____

_____

_____

_____

_____

*Additional planning and journaling space available beginning on page 75.

Something to Remember & Apply

Give to the Lord the glory *due* His name;
Bring an offering, and come into His courts.
Oh, worship the Lord in the beauty of holiness!
Tremble before Him, all the earth.

-Psalm 96:8-9

Prayer:

Father in the name of Jesus, search my heart. I want to be counted as one who can worship You in spirit and in truth. My desire is to do Your will. Help me to come up higher as I offer my worship to You. Strengthen me God, pour out boldness upon me so that I will worship even in the face of adversity.

In Jesus name, Amen.

Stirring Up Your Gifts

Everyone has heard the famously coined phrase, "It's the most wonderful time of the year," as it relates to Christmas. Yes, it is a joyous time of the year; you can feel it in the atmosphere! Christmas music playing, lights and wreaths adorning houses. Joy and anticipation shining on the faces of kids as they shake gifts under the Christmas tree wondering, *What could it be?* This is the season to give and receive gifts, but most of all, stir up your gifts. I know what you are thinking, "What does it mean to stir up my gifts?"

Wherefore I put thee in remembrance that thou stir up the gift of God, which is in thee by the putting on of my hands.
                              -2 Timothy 1:6 KJV

God has given you spiritual gifts that are to be demonstrated in your life for the continuation of the work of God. These spiritual gifts give you access to the *fullness* of life designed for you as a born-again believer. To be born again means, you have asked for forgiveness of your sins, and you are saved.

As a born-again Christian, the Holy Ghost reveals your spiritual gifts and empowers you to live an abundant life. The Holy Ghost lives in you and cultivates your gifts and brings them to maturity, so you are effective in building God's church. The spreading of the gospel of Jesus Christ must continue and God uses us, His called out separated people to do that.

I can't tell you what your specific gifts are, but I do know you have some. The wonderful thing about God, is He gave us all gifts. I don't have to imitate your gifts and you don't need to imitate my gifts.

> We have different gifts, according to the grace given to each of us. If your gift is prophesying, then prophesy in accordance with your faith; if it is serving, then serve; if it is teaching, then teach; if it is to encourage, then give encouragement; if it is giving, then give generously; if it is to lead, do it diligently; if it is to show mercy, do it cheerfully.
>
> -Romans 12:6-8 NIV

While I was reading the Bible, praying, and asking God to show me my gifts, my pastor told me we all have the gift to help. We are all called to serve. Helping aids in the building of God's kingdom.

I encourage you to ask God to reveal the gifts He has given you, so you can do your part in advancing the church. As you serve God, He is faithful to reveal your gifts. Make yourself available at home, in school, and at church. If you see a need, ask if you can help. Volunteer your time and service while you wait for your gifts to be revealed.

A Look in the Mirror

1. What are ways you can serve?

_____

_____

_____

_____

_____

_____

_____

_____

_____

2. What strengths do you see in yourself? For example, are you a good cook, administrator, or intercessor (pray for others)?

_____

_____

_____

_____

_____

_____

_____

_____

3. How do your strengths help you serve others?

_____

_____

_____

_____

_____

_____

_____

_____

_____

_____

4. Do you think it is important to serve others? Why or why not?

_____

_____

_____

_____

_____

_____

_____

_____

_____

*Additional planning and journaling space available beginning on page 75.

Something to Remember & Apply

You and your gifts are essential in God's kingdom.

As we have therefore opportunity, let us do good unto all men, especially unto them who are of the household of faith.

-Galatians 6:10 KJV

Prayer:

God, thank You for the spiritual gifts You have given me. Teach me to be sensitive to the leading of the Holy Ghost so my gifts bring You glory. God, help me to stay humble because Your word says in Proverbs 18:16, "A man's gift makes room for him, and brings him before great men." When my gifts open the doors to opportunities, help me keep Your will before me, so it accomplishes all that it was predestined to accomplish.

In the name of Jesus, Amen.

God Chose You

Doesn't it feel good to be included? Being invited to the party, picked for the team, it's an awesome feeling to know someone wants you there. I can see the smile plastered on your face, the excitement that causes you to jump up and down when you get the invitation.

It's cool to be considered and included but what happens when you are not invited, or you just don't fit in? Rejection rears its condemned head, feelings of being unworthy and inadequate creep in. In that moment, it's important to know that God chose you! He has always chosen you! You are so worthy to sit at the table He's preparing for you.

God's invitation to you is constant and unconditional. All you must do, is accept it. His invitation doesn't require you to look a certain way, dress in the latest fashion, nor come from a prestigious family. He desires you just the way you are. His invitation looks beyond what people judge as valuable.

> You did not choose me, but I chose you and appointed you so that you might go and bear fruit— fruit that will last—and so that whatever you ask in my name the Father will give you.
> -John 15:16 NIV

God not only chose you, He also gave you the opportunity to choose Him.

> This day I call the heavens and the earth as witnesses against you that I have set before you life and death, blessings and curses. Now choose life, so that you and your children may live[.]
>
> -Deuteronomy 30:19 NIV

When you make the decision to choose Jesus, it's not only good for you, but it's good for your family as well. God not only wants to bless you, but He's also concerned with those attached to you. Once you accept your invitation, God will use you to inspire others around you to accept their invitation, therefore making you an influencer for His kingdom.

A Look in the Mirror

1. When you are rejected, how do you feel?

_____

_____

_____

_____

_____

_____

_____

_____

_____

2. How do you handle rejection?

_____

_____

_____

_____

_____

_____

_____

_____

_____

_____

3. List Scriptures that reaffirm who God says you are.

_____

_____

_____

_____

_____

_____

_____

_____

_____

4. Is being chosen by God important to you? Why or why not?

_____

_____

_____

_____

_____

_____

_____

_____

*Additional planning and journaling space available beginning on page 75.

Something to Remember & Apply

But you *are* a chosen generation, a royal priesthood, a holy nation, His own special people, that you may proclaim the praises of Him who called you out of darkness into His marvelous light; who once *were* not a people but *are* now the people of God, who had not obtained mercy but now have obtained mercy.

-1 Peter 2:9-10

Prayer:

Thank You God, for choosing me. I know I am accepted in the beloved. I renounce fear, rejection, and feelings of being unworthy. Help me to know that You are my portion and if no one else includes me, You have already chosen me. God, I commit my feelings and emotions into Your hand. I am content as Your child.

In the name of Jesus, Amen.

Invitation to Christ

We have spent several months reviewing and reading about the goodness of God. I pray you have gained some insight that will take you further in life. I pray, each month you have partnered with the Holy Spirit to grow in your walk with Christ. If at any point, you felt or heard the Lord calling you to be saved, repeat this prayer:

God, forgive me for the sins I have committed. I believe and accept the finish work of Jesus Christ. He died on the cross for my sins. Jesus, come into my heart and teach me to live for You.

If you prayed that prayer and believed it in your heart, you are saved. Salvation is that simple. God has given you a new start. Connect with a church that preaches and teaches the good news of Jesus!

God bless you.

But what does it say? "The word is near you, in your mouth and in your heart" (that is, the word of faith which we preach): that if you confess with your mouth the Lord Jesus and believe in your heart that God has raised Him from the dead, you will be saved. For with the heart one believes unto righteousness, and with the mouth confession is made unto salvation.

-Romans 10:8-10

About the Author

Dynisha Warren-Fresneda was born in Pahokee, a small city located in beautiful sunny South Florida. Dynisha considers her faith and family to be the most important to her. She's an entrepreneur and a Registered Nurse. If she isn't spending time with her family and friends, you can almost always find her working in her community, training the next generation of compassionate healthcare workers.

Dynisha is the cofounder and operator of Victory Nursing Inc.

Compassion • Integrity • Excellence

This prestigious one-training program currently offers Certified Nursing Assistant (CNA) training by Registered Nurses. The school was established in 2019 by a mother and daughter team who are both passionate about the nursing profession.

Stay Connected:

Please email Dynisha to schedule speaking engagements or book shares. Bulk book discounts are available for small group leaders and mentors.

dynisha.warren146@gmail.com

Is God directing you into the healthcare field? Please email me for more information about Victory Nursing Inc.

victorynursing.2019@gmail.com

Planning & Journaling

[F]or all have sinned and fall short of the glory of God,
-Romans 3:23

_____

_____

_____

_____

_____

_____

_____

_____

_____

_____

_____

_____

_____

_____

_____

_____

_____

_____

_____

_____

_____

_____

_____

_____

*For we must all appear before the judgment seat of Christ,
that each one may receive the things done in the body,
according to what he has done, whether good or bad.*
-2 Corinthians 5:10

_____

_____

_____

_____

_____

_____

_____

_____

_____

_____

_____

_____

_____

_____

_____

_____

_____

_____

_____

_____

_____

_____

*But the word is very near you, in your mouth and
in your heart, that you may do it.*
-Deuteronomy 30:14

_____

_____

_____

_____

_____

_____

_____

_____

_____

_____

_____

_____

_____

_____

_____

_____

_____

_____

_____

_____

_____

_____

_____

For the wages of sin is death, but the gift of God is eternal life in Christ Jesus our Lord.
-Romans 6:23

The Lord is not slack concerning His promise, as some count slackness, but is longsuffering toward us, not willing that any should perish but that all should come to repentance.

-2 Peter 3:9

Truly, these times of ignorance God overlooked,
but now commands all men everywhere to repent,
-Acts 17:30

For we are His workmanship, created in Christ Jesus for good works, which God prepared beforehand that we should walk in them.
-Ephesians 2:10

O Lord, You have searched me and known me.
You know my sitting down and my rising up;
You understand my thought afar off.
-Psalm 139:1-2

Now then, we are ambassadors for Christ, as though God
were pleading through us: we implore you on
Christ's behalf, be reconciled to God.
-2 Corinthians 5:20

I can do all things through Christ who strengthens me.
-Philippians 4:13

There is therefore now no condemnation to those who are in Christ Jesus, who do not walk according to the flesh, but according to the Spirit.
-Romans 8:1

_____

_____

_____

_____

_____

_____

_____

_____

_____

_____

_____

_____

_____

_____

_____

_____

_____

_____

_____

_____

_____

_____

_____

_____

Yet in all these things we are more than conquerors
through Him who loved us.
-*Romans 8:37*

_____

_____

_____

_____

_____

_____

_____

_____

_____

_____

_____

_____

_____

_____

_____

_____

_____

_____

_____

_____

_____

"For you are a holy people to the Lord your God; the Lord your God has chosen you to be a people for Himself, a special treasure above all the peoples on the face of the earth.
-Deuteronomy 7:6

_____

_____

_____

_____

_____

_____

_____

_____

_____

_____

_____

_____

_____

_____

_____

_____

_____

_____

_____

_____

_____

_____

_____

Monthly Calendars

Month / Year

Sun.	Mon.	Tues.	Wed.	Thurs.	Fri.	Sat.

My goal for this month: _____

Strategy to meet my goal: _____
_____
_____

How I will mark my progress: _____
_____
_____

Do I need to pivot to better meet my goal? If so, explain how: _____
_____
_____

A positive affirmation to myself: _____
_____

Notes:

Month / Year

_____

Sun.	Mon.	Tues.	Wed.	Thurs.	Fri.	Sat.

My goal for this month: _____

Strategy to meet my goal: _____
_____
_____

How I will mark my progress: _____
_____
_____

Do I need to pivot to better meet my goal? If so, explain how: _____
_____
_____

A positive affirmation to myself: _____
_____

Notes:

_____

_____

_____

_____

_____

_____

_____

_____

_____

_____

_____

_____

_____

_____

_____

_____

_____

_____

_____

_____

_____

_____

_____

_____

_____

_____

_____

Month / Year

_____

Sun.	Mon.	Tues.	Wed.	Thurs.	Fri.	Sat.

My goal for this month: _____

Strategy to meet my goal: _____
_____
_____

How I will mark my progress: _____
_____
_____

Do I need to pivot to better meet my goal? If so, explain how: _____
_____
_____

A positive affirmation to myself: _____
_____

Notes:

Month / Year

_____

Sun.	Mon.	Tues.	Wed.	Thurs.	Fri.	Sat.

My goal for this month: _____

Strategy to meet my goal: _____
_____
_____

How I will mark my progress: _____
_____
_____

Do I need to pivot to better meet my goal? If so, explain how: _____
_____
_____

A positive affirmation to myself: _____
_____

Notes:

_____

_____

_____

_____

_____

_____

_____

_____

_____

_____

_____

_____

_____

_____

_____

_____

_____

_____

_____

_____

_____

_____

_____

_____

_____

_____

_____

_____

_____

Month / Year

Sun.	Mon.	Tues.	Wed.	Thurs.	Fri.	Sat.

My goal for this month: _____

Strategy to meet my goal: _____
_____
_____

How I will mark my progress: _____
_____
_____

Do I need to pivot to better meet my goal? If so, explain how: _____
_____
_____

A positive affirmation to myself: _____
_____

Notes:

Month / Year

_____

Sun.	Mon.	Tues.	Wed.	Thurs.	Fri.	Sat.

My goal for this month: _____

Strategy to meet my goal: _____
_____
_____

How I will mark my progress: _____
_____
_____

Do I need to pivot to better meet my goal? If so, explain how: _____
_____
_____

A positive affirmation to myself: _____
_____

Notes:

Month / Year

_____

Sun.	Mon.	Tues.	Wed.	Thurs.	Fri.	Sat.

My goal for this month: _____

Strategy to meet my goal: _____
_____
_____

How I will mark my progress: _____
_____
_____

Do I need to pivot to better meet my goal? If so, explain how: _____
_____
_____

A positive affirmation to myself: _____
_____

Notes:

Month / Year

_____

Sun.	Mon.	Tues.	Wed.	Thurs.	Fri.	Sat.

My goal for this month: _____

Strategy to meet my goal: _____
_____
_____

How I will mark my progress: _____
_____
_____

Do I need to pivot to better meet my goal? If so, explain how: _____
_____
_____

A positive affirmation to myself: _____
_____

Notes:

Month / Year

_____

Sun.	Mon.	Tues.	Wed.	Thurs.	Fri.	Sat.

My goal for this month: _____

Strategy to meet my goal: _____
_____
_____

How I will mark my progress: _____
_____
_____

Do I need to pivot to better meet my goal? If so, explain
how: _____
_____
_____

A positive affirmation to myself: _____
_____

Notes:

_____
_____
_____
_____
_____
_____
_____
_____
_____
_____
_____
_____
_____
_____
_____
_____
_____
_____
_____
_____
_____
_____
_____
_____
_____
_____
_____

Month / Year

_____

Sun.	Mon.	Tues.	Wed.	Thurs.	Fri.	Sat.

My goal for this month: _____

Strategy to meet my goal: _____
_____
_____

How I will mark my progress: _____
_____
_____

Do I need to pivot to better meet my goal? If so, explain how: _____
_____
_____

A positive affirmation to myself: _____
_____

Notes:

Month / Year

_____

Sun.	Mon.	Tues.	Wed.	Thurs.	Fri.	Sat.

My goal for this month: _____

Strategy to meet my goal: _____
_____
_____

How I will mark my progress: _____
_____
_____

Do I need to pivot to better meet my goal? If so, explain
how: _____
_____
_____

A positive affirmation to myself: _____
_____

Notes:

Month / Year

Sun.	Mon.	Tues.	Wed.	Thurs.	Fri.	Sat.

My goal for this month: _____

Strategy to meet my goal: _____
_____
_____

How I will mark my progress: _____
_____
_____

Do I need to pivot to better meet my goal? If so, explain how: _____
_____
_____

A positive affirmation to myself: _____
_____

Notes:

www.ingramcontent.com/pod-product-compliance
Lightning Source LLC
Chambersburg PA
CBHW071013120626
46546CB00003B/1075